I0489819

Rejection of perfection and my approach.

Digital photography has given the majority of the world access to a camera. A camera that captures clean, sterile, and even perfect replications of the subjects it's pointed at. As precise as that image may arguably be, my process and my photographic work seeks to be imperfect, unclean, almost ugly and embrace the qualities that make 35mm film what it is, in all its grainy glory.I am not trying to find beauty or perfection; I'm searching for something real in a society that continuously shifts toward a synthetic truth.I cannot tell you what to see when you look through my work, I can only offer them to you and hope that you see something in them yourself. What they say to you is what they mean.

My Heart's Not Beating As It Should is a photo textual narrative short about one person's psychological difficulties navigating human interactions while suffering from poor body confidence, social anxiety, and neurodiversity. Rory Chapman represents this struggle through subtly surreal photographic imagery an imperfect poetry.

For more work by Rory Chapman, please visit:

www.rorychapman.com

Ok, stay calm. Smile.

Not too much.

Eye contact for 3 seconds
Don't look down, you know what they'll think if you do.

How's my posture?

Think me feet are pointing the wrong way again.

Better turn them the other direction.

Don't want to give them the wrong idea.

You just looked down. Damn it!

Look somewhere else for a bit.

No that's too long, now you look disinterested.

JUST PRETEND EVERYTHING IS FINE.

Oh, thank God they've gone.

I need another drink...

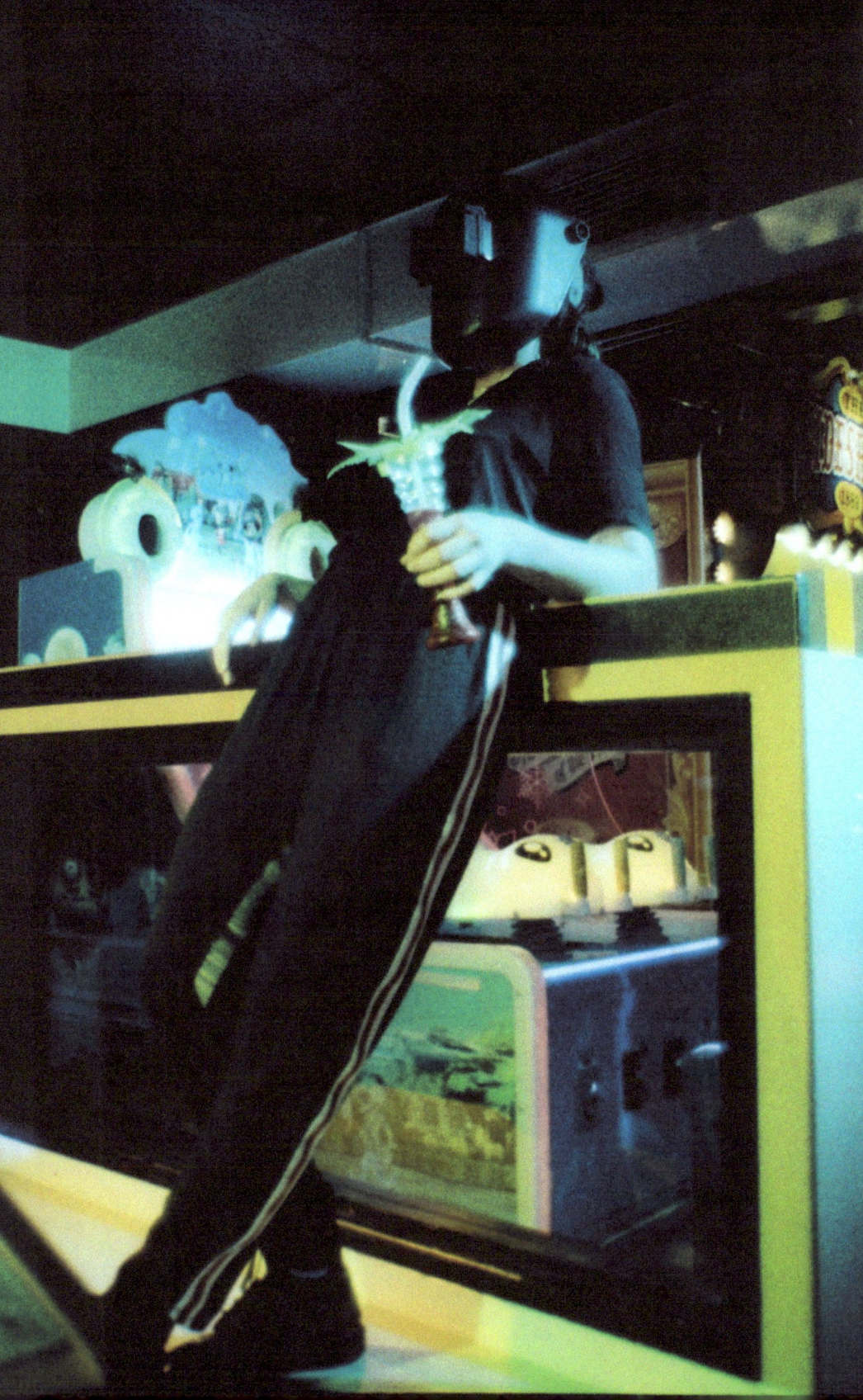

RELAXED. LEANING ON A RAILING

I'VE SEEN PEOPLE DO THIS.

THIS IS CORRECT. RIGHT?

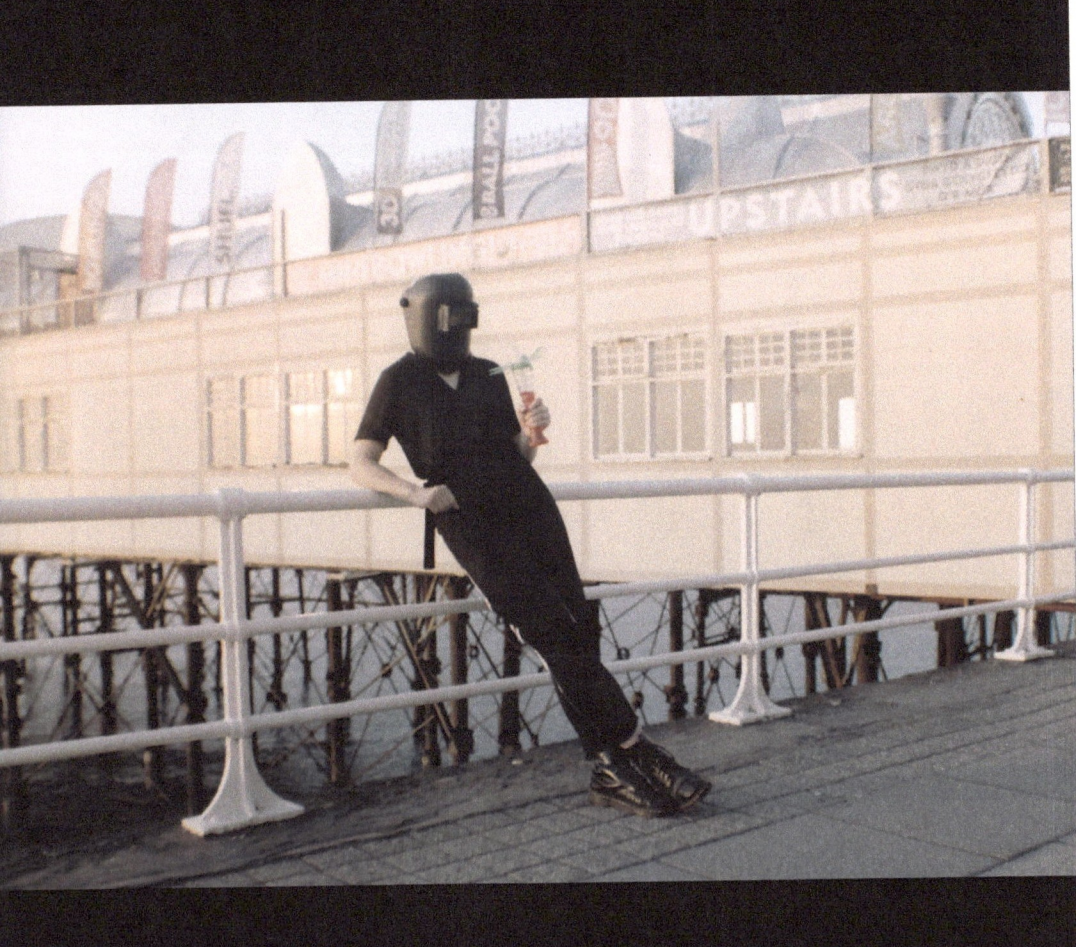

try to look Normal, try to look Normal,

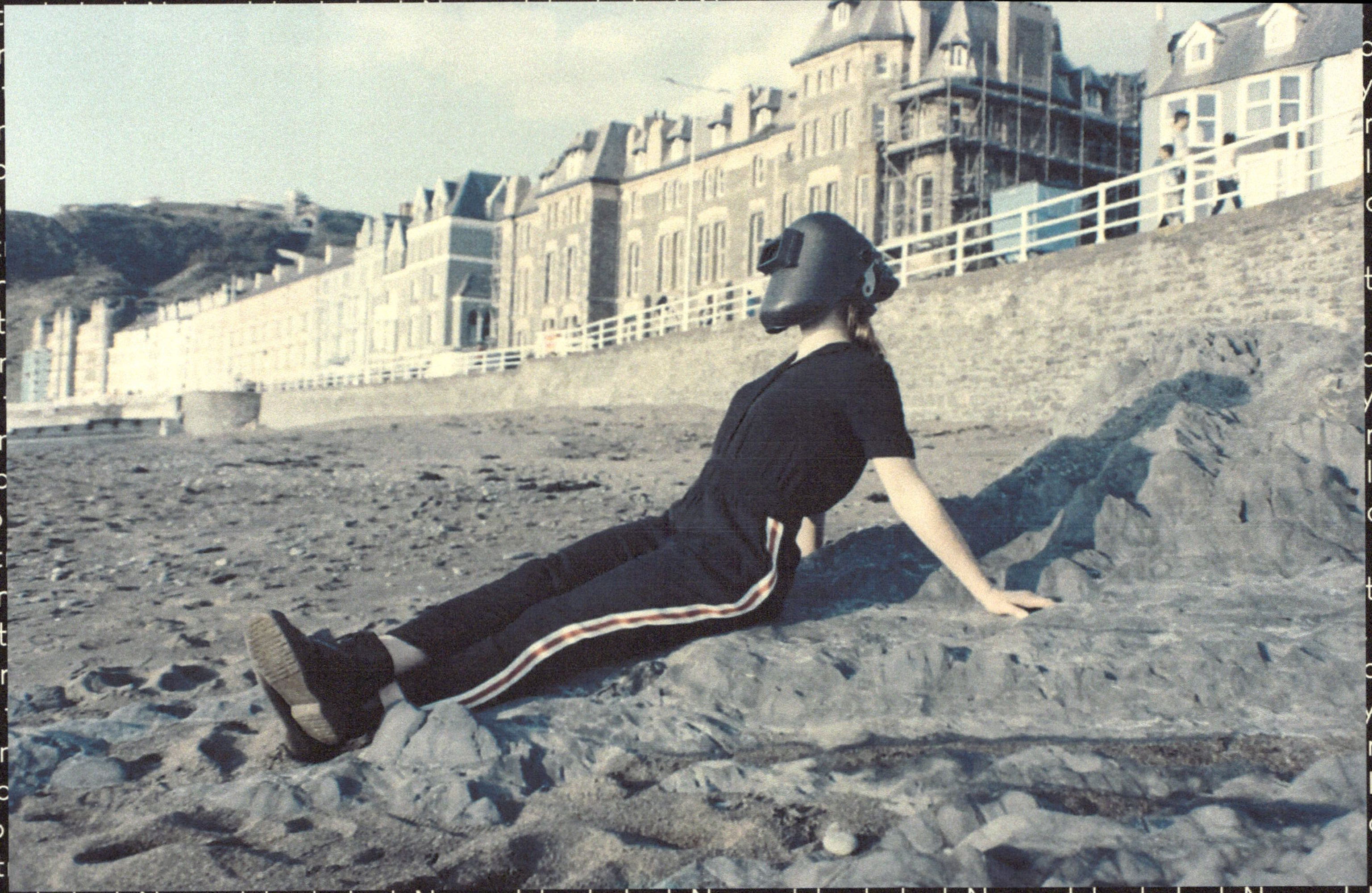

rmal, try to look Normal, try to look Normal, try to look Normal, try to look Normal, try to look Normal, try to
rmal, try to look Normal, try to look Normal, try to look Normal, try to look Normal, try to look Normal, try to

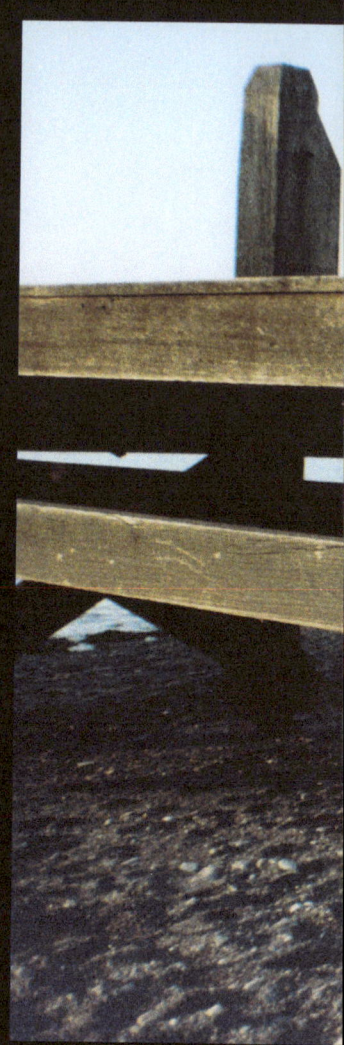

NAILED IT

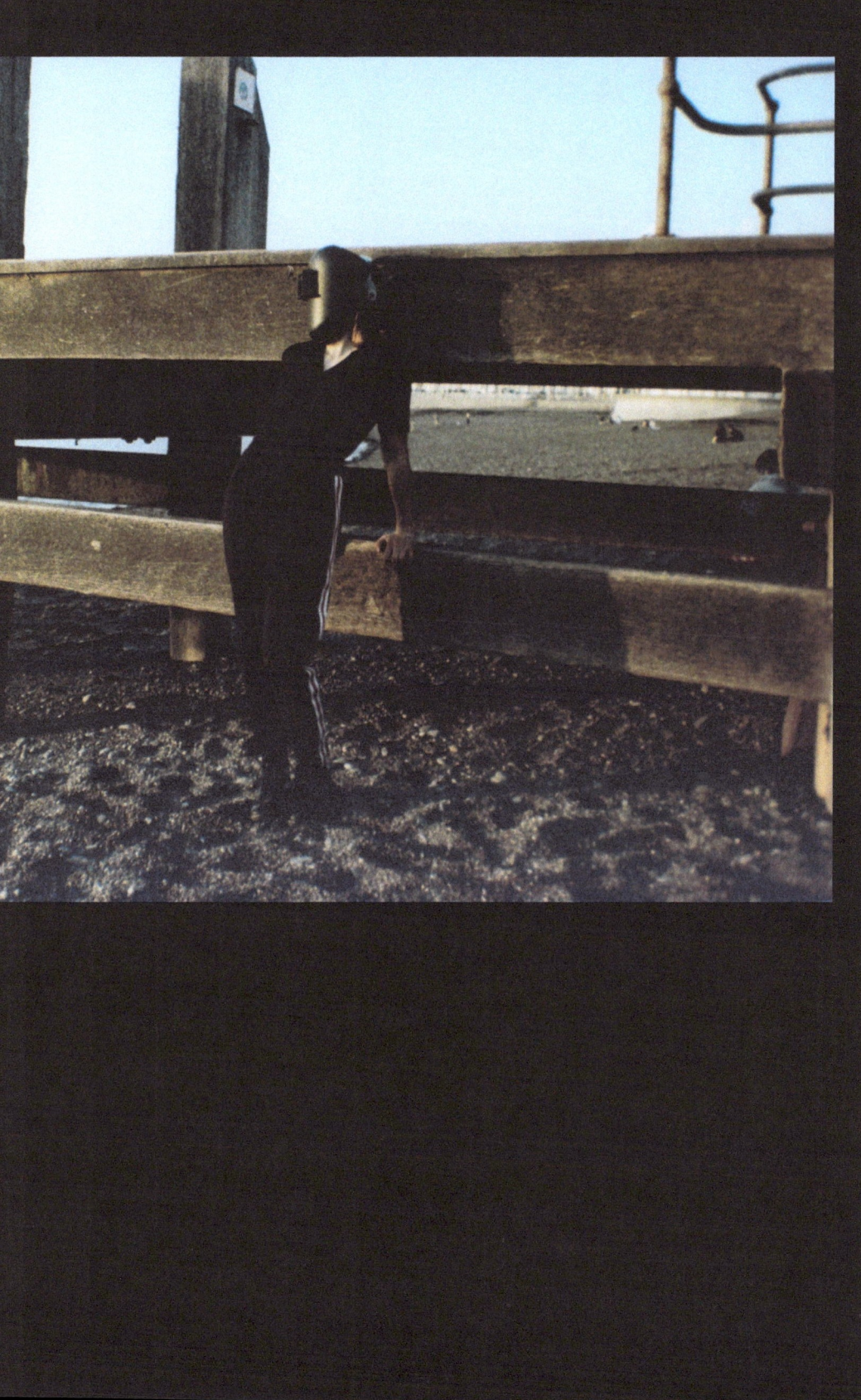

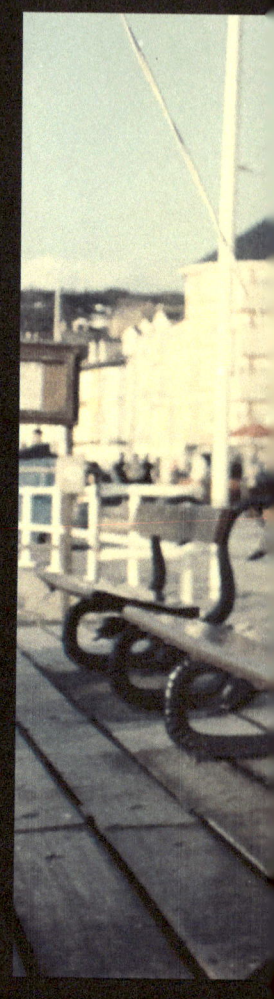

Just enjoy it.

It's only a little bit of heat, it won't last long

JUST BE COOL.

No one will notice.

Everything is ok.

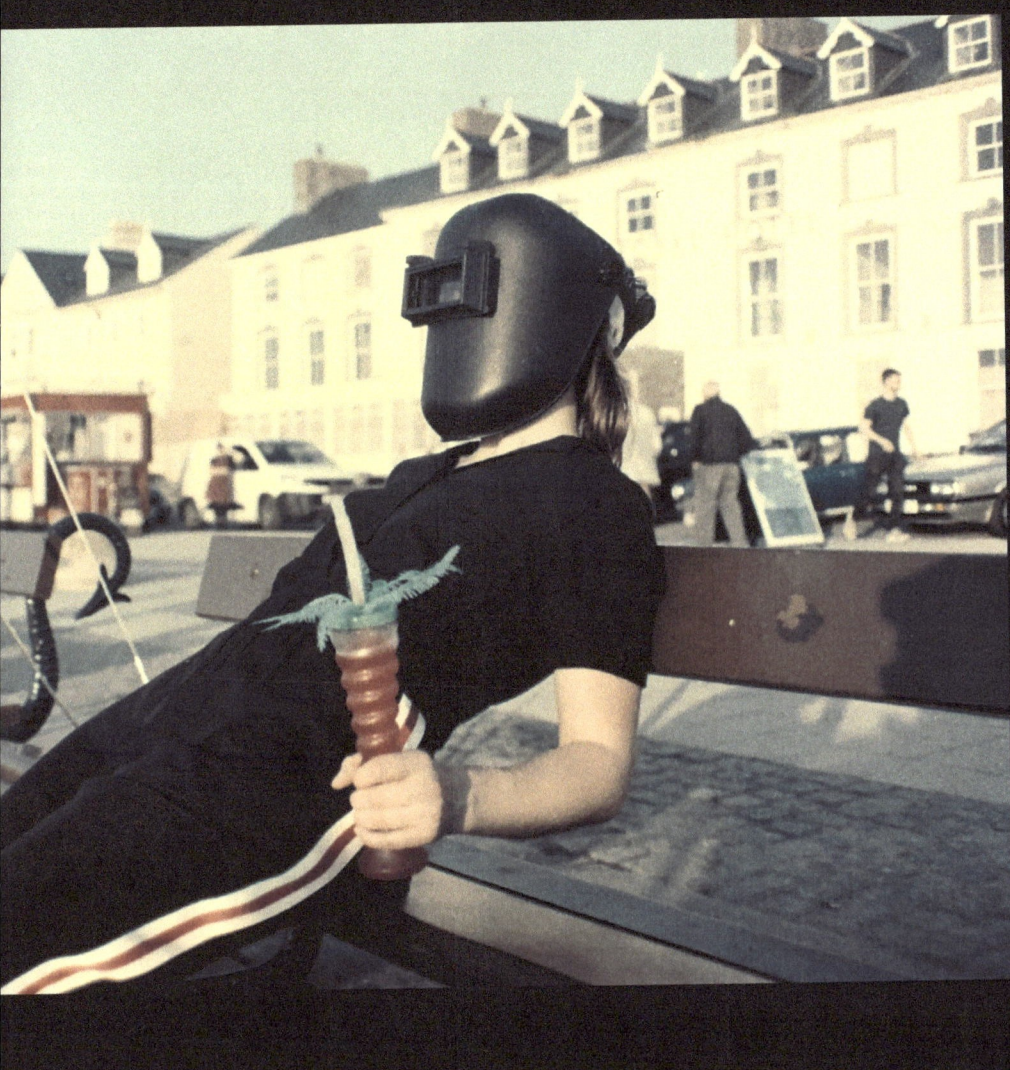

My blood is like honey,

So thick it's stuck in my chest.

MY HEART'S NOT BEATING AS IT SHOULD.

Feels like dying.

I need to leave, but everyone's having fun.

Am I dying... I think I'm dying.

How hot can a person get before I have a seizure?

My heart's not beating as it should, and I can't tell anyone

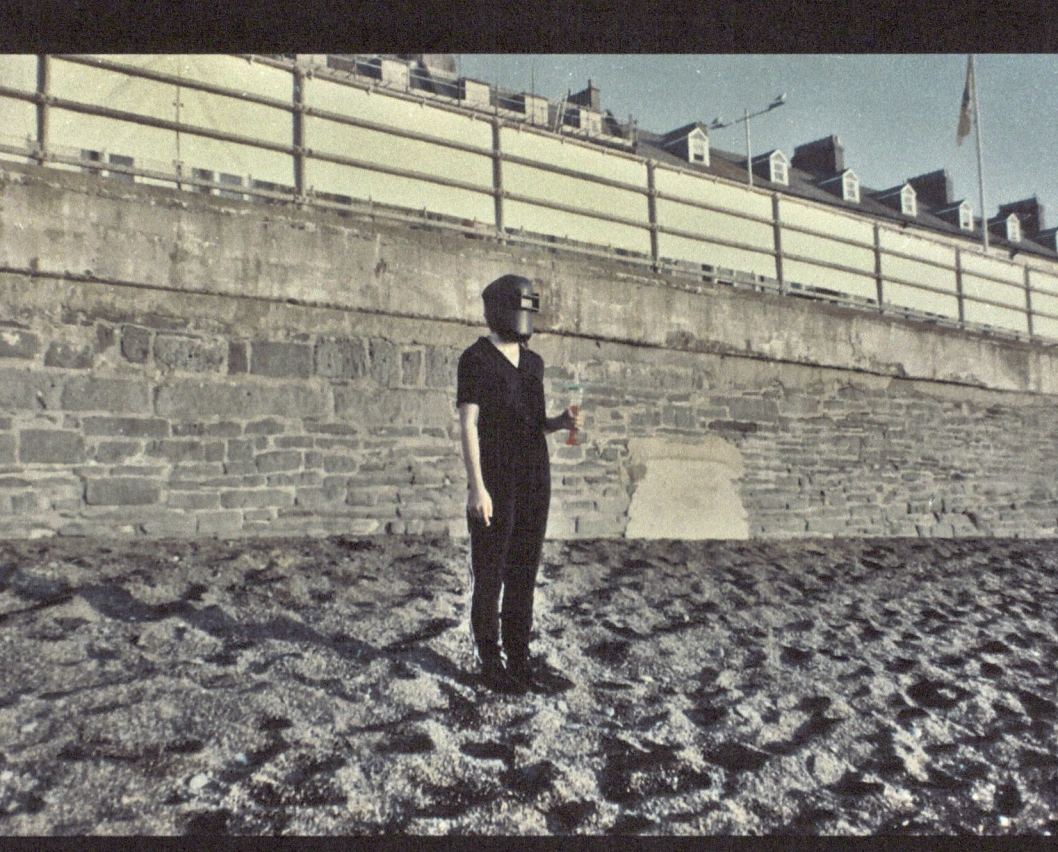

Maybe the heat will sweat the fat off.

Maybe the sun will cook the juices,

and soak up in my clothes.

BURN ME ALL DOWN.

Burn me until I'm not there no more.

Dust. Blackened dust.

Burn me all down.

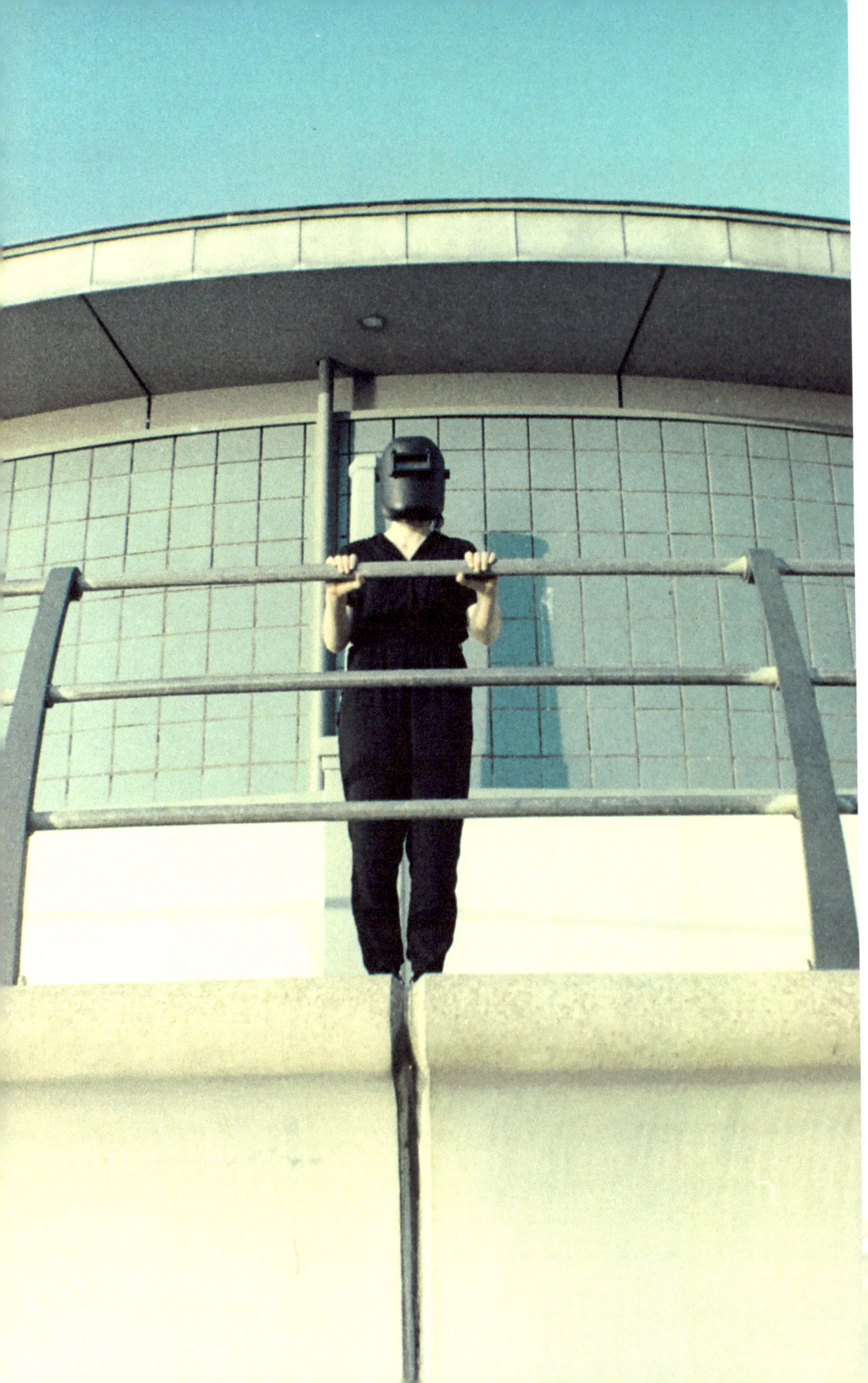

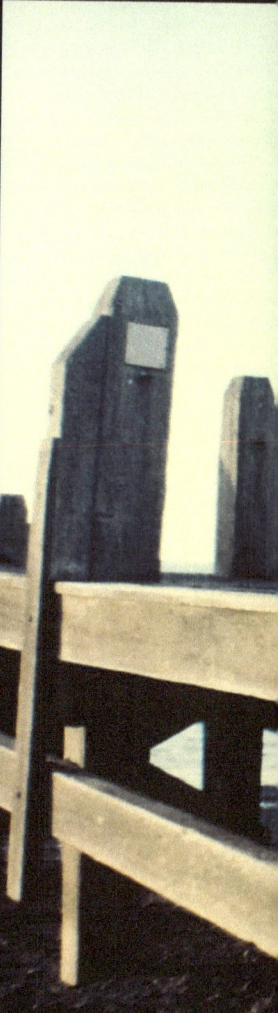

It's coming, I can feel it...
The end is in sight now.
The blood has stopped moving in my veins,
My heart, no longer beating at a rhythmical pace,
My pours devoid of moisture to cool my skin.
This is it, it's coming...
I SWEAR I'LL DIE TO THIS.
It's only a matter of time now.

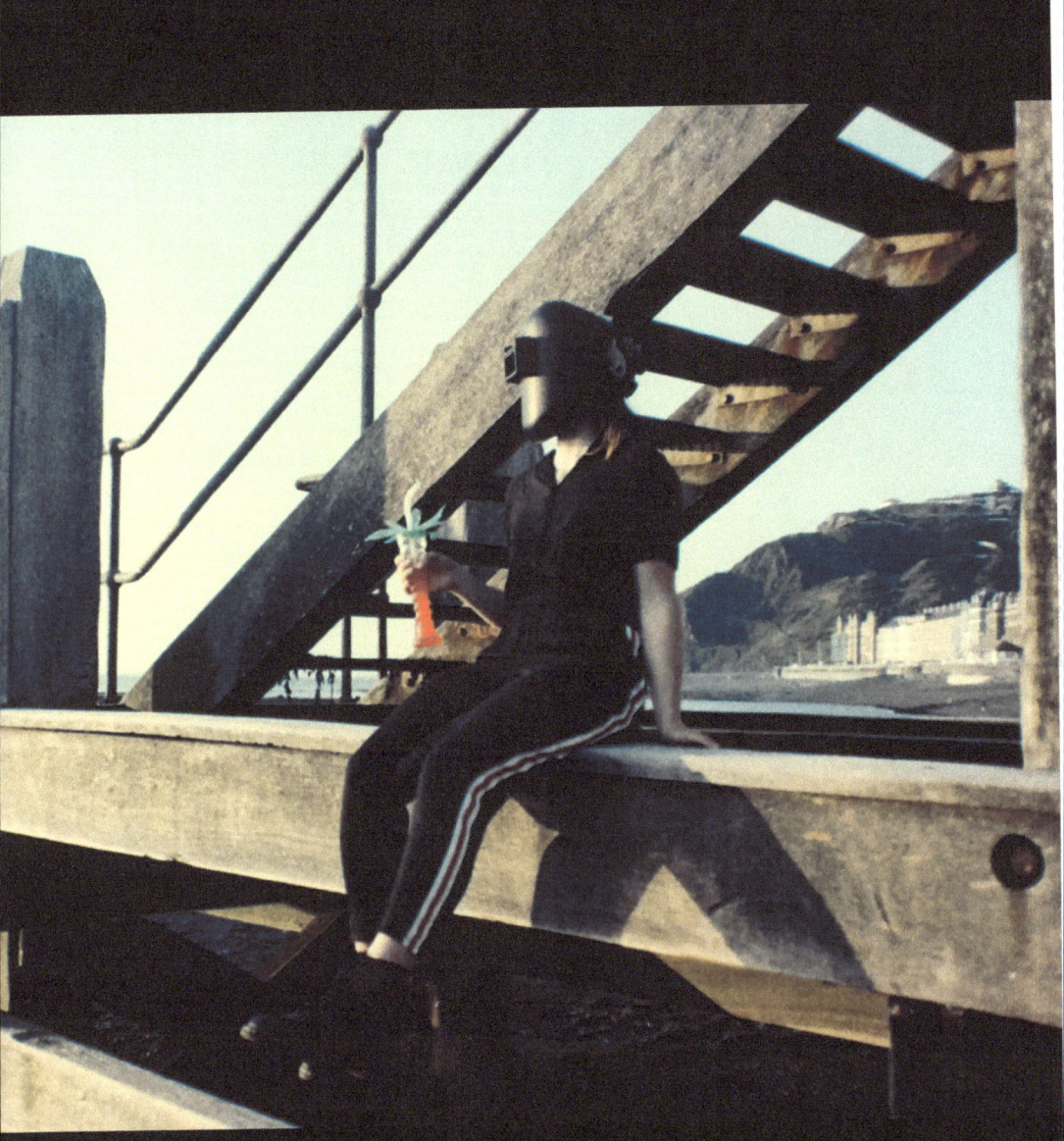

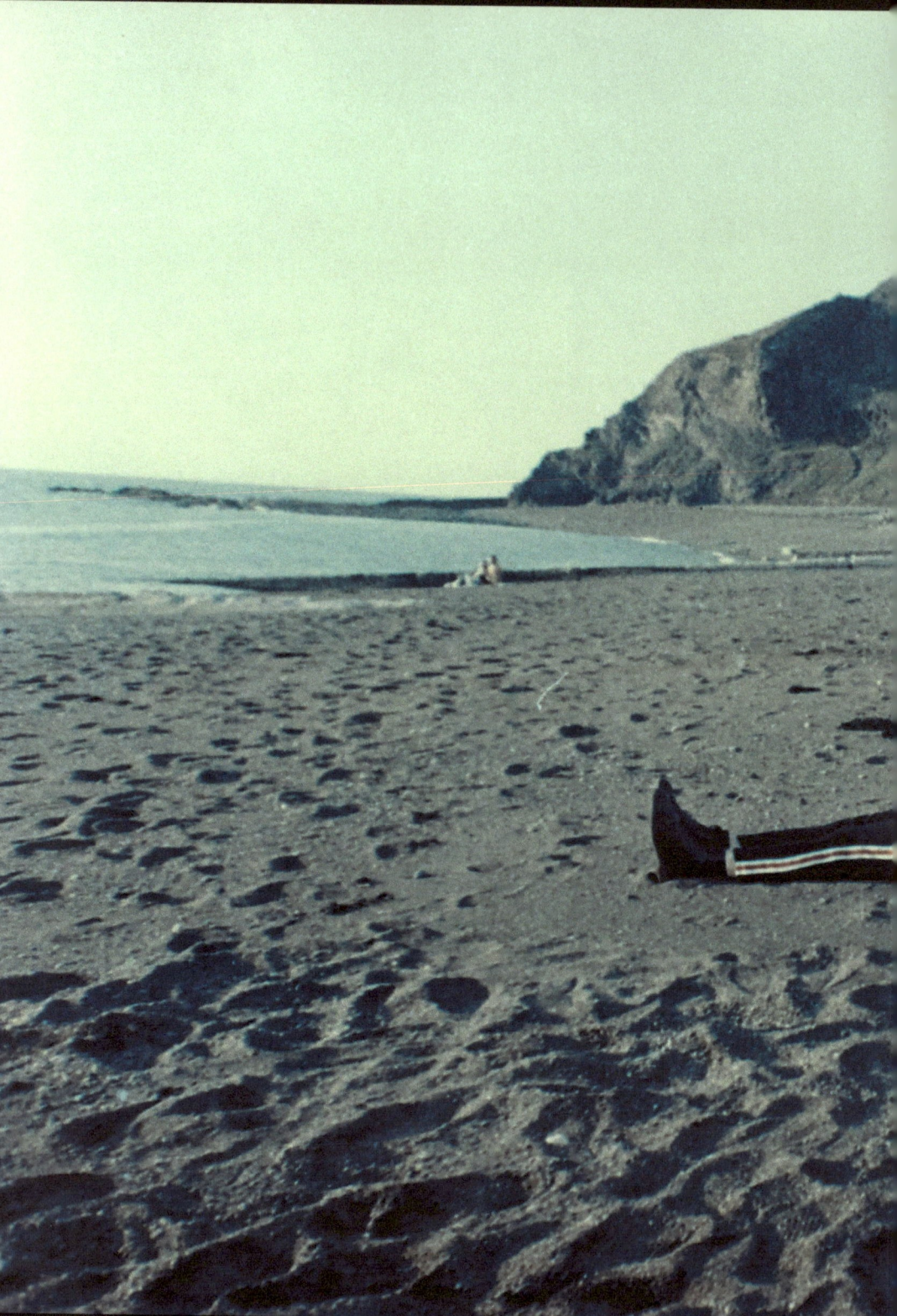

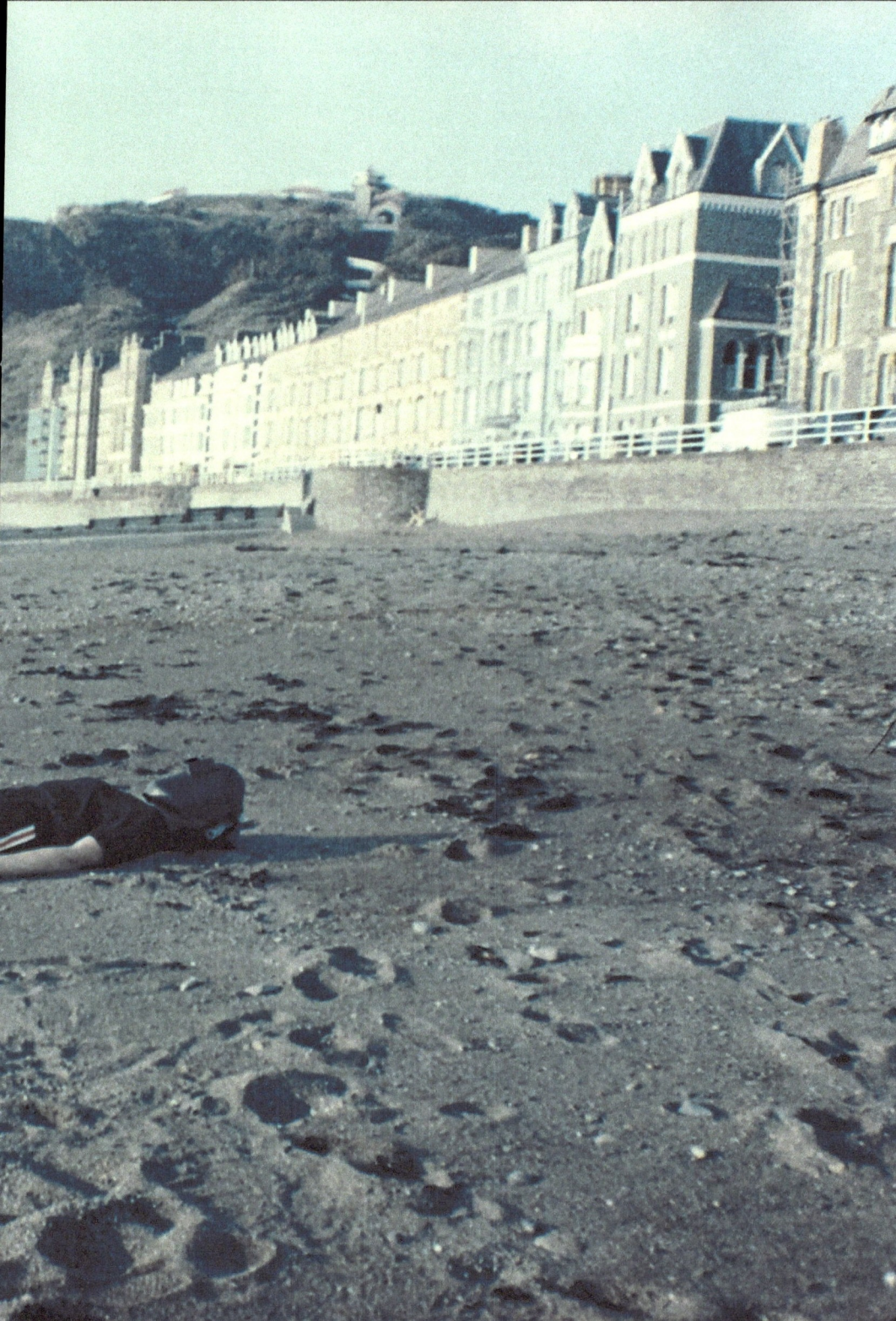

Technical Information

Camera: Chinon CM-3 SLR

Lens: Optimax 35mm f2.8

Film stock: Wolfen NC500

Developer: BelliniFoto C41 kit

Location: Aberystwyth beach, Wales, UK

Model: Bronwen Hull

Date: Summer 2023

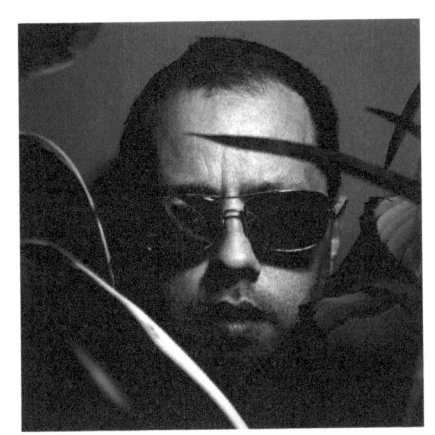